# pumpkin butternut & squash

# pumpkin butternut & squash

## 30 sweet and savory recipes

**Elsa Petersen-Schepelern**

photography by **Debi Treloar**

RYLAND
PETERS
& SMALL
LONDON NEW YORK

**For my brother-in-law Ron Bray the pumpkin guru!**

| | |
|---|---|
| Senior Designer | Ashley Western |
| Editor | Maddalena Bastianelli |
| Production | Patricia Harrington |
| Art Director | Gabriella Le Grazie |
| Publishing Director | Alison Starling |
| | |
| Food Stylist | Maxine Clark |
| Cooking Assistant | Kate Habershon |
| Stylist | Rebecca Duke |
| Photographer's Assistant | Kate Peters |

**Author's acknowledgments:**
My thanks to my sister Kirsten, to Peter and Trish Bray, Abbie Stürmer, Luc Votan
(for his expert advice on Vietnamese food), and to Trish Peters for turning New York
upside down in pursuit of pumpkins and squash. Thanks also to friends Maddie
Bastianelli and Sheridan Lear for helping with recipe testing, Tara McCarthy,
pumpkin-pie-cook *par excellence*—and to Zia Mattocks, the "Curry Queen."
Thanks also to Maxine Clarke for her delicious food styling, Kate Habershon
for her utter unflappability, and Debi Treloar for her lush photography.

**Notes:**
All spoon measurements are level unless otherwise stated.
Grills, ovens, and broilers should be heated to the required temperature before
adding the food. If using a convection oven, adjust cooking times according to
the manufacturer's instructions.
Specialty Asian ingredients are available in large supermarkets, Thai, Chinese,
Japanese, and Vietnamese shops, as well as Asian stores.

First published in the USA in 2000
This edition published 2003
by Ryland Peters & Small, Inc.
519 Broadway, 5th Floor
New York, NY 10012
www.rylandpeters.com

10 9 8 7 6 5 4 3 2

Text © Elsa Petersen-Schepelern 2000
Design and photographs © Ryland Peters & Small 2000

ISBN 1 84172 527 7

Printed and bound in China

Library of Congress Cataloging-in-Publication Data

Petersen-Schepelern, Elsa.
  Pumpkin, butternut & squash : 30 sweet and savory recipes / Elsa
Petersen-Schepelern ; photography by Debi Treloar.
    p. cm.
Includes index.
  ISBN 1-84172-527-7
  1. Cookery (Pumpkin) 2. Cookery (Squash)  I. Title.
TX803.P93P48 2003
641.6'562--dc21

                                              2003005701

# there's more to a pumpkin than a lantern...

Pumpkins, butternuts, and squash—all of which originate in America—are much loved vegetables all over the world, as the recipes in this book will show.

The question is which of this huge tribe are we going to use for a particular dish? Perhaps some of the most familiar are the bright orange pumpkins used for jack o' lanterns at Halloween. Very nice they are too—for lanterns. But for the true pumpkin aficionado, the best for cooking are those with blue-gray, gray, or dark green skin and a brilliant orange interior—they have dense, mealy flesh, full of sweetness and flavor.

And that's the key. The very sweetness of pumpkin has given him an identity crisis. Is he sweet or is he savory? The answer is both.

Pumpkin's squashy cousins include the ubiquitous butternut squash—with its elongated neck, pale orange flesh, and sweet, delicious flavor, it is available in almost every supermarket.

Then there are the pretty pattypans and the familiar zucchini, sweet and juicy. (But please—the name zucchini means that it should be tiny. If it's big, it's not half so nice.) Personally, I prefer zucchinis finely sliced and uncooked—in salads—or minimally cooked and doused in dressing.

Other delicious morsels include the acorn squash, with dark green segmented hide, and little golden "sugar pumpkins," wonderful stuffed.

Even sweeter and juicier is the chayote, also known as the choko, chow-chow, christophine, or mirliton—which deserves to be better known. He has a pale green skin and is about the size and shape of a pear. Where I grew up, he was so common he was positively despised. I never knew why.

# snacks and salads

# zucchini and pattypan salad
## with pumpkin seed oil dressing

Pumpkin seed oil—dark olive green and deliciously nutty—is an absolute treat. Use sparingly and serve lime wedges separately so people can add the juice to taste. Once you've tasted pumpkin seed oil, I promise you it's addictive. I prefer to microwave all the vegetables for this salad to keep them *al dente*.

6 oz. asparagus tips
6 oz. green beans
1½ cups shelled green peas, frozen or fresh
8 baby zucchinis, halved lengthways
1½ cups sugarsnap peas
4 pattypan squash, finely sliced on
    a mandoline
2 tablespoons olive oil
sea salt and freshly ground black pepper

**TO SERVE:**
3 tablespoons pumpkin seed oil
2 limes, cut into wedges
small sprigs of fresh mint

SERVES 4

Half-fill a large bowl with ice cubes, then add cold water to three-quarters full. Set aside.

Cook the asparagus until *al dente* (firm in the middle)—microwave on HIGH for 1 minute if small, 1½ minutes if large, or boil or steam for about 6 minutes. Remove immediately from the heat, drain, and plunge immediately into the ice water. Leave until ice cold.

Do the same with the green beans (for 2/6 minutes), green peas, and zucchinis (1/3 minutes), and sugarsnaps (30 seconds/1 minute), plunging immediately into the ice water. The asparagus, peas, zucchinis, and beans should be cooked, but still firm. Drain well, pat dry with paper towels, and put in a bowl. Add the sliced pattypans, olive oil, salt, and pepper and toss gently until coated.

Transfer to a chilled salad serving dish or 4 individual plates. Drizzle with pumpkin seed oil and serve with wedges of lime and sprigs of mint.

# roasted pumpkin salad
## with red onions and lentils

A filling salad that's good for lunch. I like it with Puy lentils, or the yellow ones from Indian shops called channa dal. The watercress is optional, but I find it gives a peppery crunch.

Put the pumpkin or butternut cubes, garlic cloves, and onion quarters in a plastic bag, add the salt and paprika, and shake until well covered. Add half the olive oil and shake again.

Brush a roasting pan with 1 tablespoon of the oil, then arrange the pumpkin or butternut, garlic, and onions over the base. Add the tomatoes, brush with oil, and prick the tops with a toothpick. Trickle 1–2 tablespoons oil over the top and sprinkle with salt and pepper.

Roast in a preheated oven at 400°F for 10 minutes, then remove the tomatoes just as the skins begin to split. Continue roasting until the onions and pumpkin or butternut are tender.

Remove from the oven and divide between 4 salad plates. To each plate add 2 tablespoons cooked Puy lentils, a quarter of the goat cheese, and 2 of the anchovy fillets. Sprinkle with lemon juice and about 2–4 teaspoons olive oil, then salt and freshly ground black pepper. Add sprigs of watercress, if using, and serve.

¼ small pumpkin or ½ butternut squash, peeled, seeded, and cut into 1-inch cubes
4 garlic cloves, peeled and speared on a bamboo satay stick
4 small red onions, quartered lengthwise through the root
1 teaspoon sea salt
1 tablespoon hot paprika
¼–⅓ cup extra virgin olive oil
about 24 cherry tomatoes
1 cup cooked Puy lentils, about 4 oz.
1 organic goat cheese, about 4 oz., crumbled
8 anchovy fillets
freshly squeezed juice of 1 large lemon
sea salt flakes and freshly ground black pepper
8–12 large sprigs of watercress (optional)

SERVES 4

# crispy indian pakoras
## with pumpkins, zucchinis, and chiles

The Indian version of the Japanese tempura is the bhaji or pakora. These favorite Indian fritters can be made of many kinds of vegetable—you might like to serve a selection of different kinds at a party. They are delicious served with a spicy coconut chutney or mint and cucumber raita.

6 oz. pumpkin, cut into ⅛-inch slices
2 onions, halved and sliced
8 baby zucchinis, finely sliced lengthwise
4 mild red chiles, halved lengthwise, and seeded
4 zucchini flowers (optional)
peanut or sunflower oil, for frying

**PAKORA BATTER:**
1⅓ cups chickpea flour (gram flour or besan)
½ teaspoon baking soda
½ teaspoon chili powder
2 teaspoons ajwain powder, or ground fennel seeds or celery seeds
a pinch of salt

**CUCUMBER AND MINT RAITA:**
1 cup plain yogurt
1 small cucumber, about 6–8 inches long
a pinch of ground cumin
1 teaspoon sugar
1 teaspoon freshly squeezed lemon juice
a handful of fresh mint leaves, chopped
salt

SERVES 4

To make the raita, line a strainer with cheesecloth, add the yogurt, and let drain for about 30 minutes. Quarter the cucumber lengthwise, then slice finely. Sprinkle with salt, set aside for 10–30 minutes, then drain and pat dry with paper towels. Put the strained yogurt in a bowl and beat with an electric beater or whisk until slightly thickened. Beat in the cumin and sugar. Fold through the cucumber, lemon juice, and mint, chill for at least 30 minutes, then serve.

To make the batter, sift the chickpea flour, baking soda, and salt into a large bowl, then stir in the chili powder and ground ajwain, fennel, or celery. Add about ¾ cup cold water to make a loose batter.

Fill a wok or kettle one-third full of the oil or a deep-fryer to the manufacturer's recommended level. Heat to 375°F or until a cube of bread browns in 30 seconds. Working in batches, dip the pumpkin slices in the batter and fry in a single layer until lightly golden. Remove with a slotted spoon and drain on crumpled paper towels. Keep them hot in the oven while you cook the other vegetables.

Repeat with the remaining vegetables (To cook the onions and zucchinis, take make small bundles of about 6 slices each and cook them in the bundles.)

Serve hot, with the Cucumber and Mint Raita.

# pumpkin seed granola

A friend in Sydney turns even health food like this into a gourmet experience. You choose how much sweetening to use (if any) and include your favorite grains—some people like soft oats, others prefer the crunch of toasted buckwheat (have lots of the things you like and none of those you don't). Serve it with milk like ordinary cereal—or like the Swiss do, with yogurt and even stewed fruit.

Put the pumpkin and sunflower seeds in a food processor and pulse to chop coarsely. Put in a dry skillet and heat until lightly toasted but not browned. Transfer to a large pitcher or bowl and let cool.

Put all the nuts in a food processor and pulse to chop coarsely. Put in the dry skillet, add the coconut, if using, and heat until lightly toasted but not browned. Transfer to the pitcher and let cool.

Add the oats or oatmeal, oat bran, toasted buckwheat, if using, plus all the dried fruits to the pitcher. Stir well, then transfer to an airtight container. If keeping for longer than a few days, store in the refrigerator to prevent the oils in the nuts and seeds from developing "off" tastes.

Serve with milk or yogurt, plus honey or sugar if preferred (I find it doesn't need sweetening because of the dried fruit).

**Variation:** Fresh or stewed fruit is also a delicious accompaniment.

½ cup pumpkin seeds*
½ cup sunflower seeds
½ cup flaked almonds
½ cup cashews
2 tablespoons unsweetened shredded coconut (optional)
2⅔ cups rolled oats or medium oatmeal
1 cup oat bran
2 tablespoons toasted buckwheat (optional)
½ cup dried fruit such as figs, mango, papaya or banana, chopped
½ cup raisins
½ cup dried apple rings, chopped

**TO SERVE:**
skimmed milk or plain yogurt
honey or sugar, to taste (optional)

MAKES ABOUT 8 SERVINGS

**\*Note**: If you like, use your own roasted butternut seeds (page 17), but omit the salt, oil, dried chiles, and chili powder when toasting.

# spicy caribbean chips

## of pumpkin, plantain, and sweet potato

A favorite treat for a party—serve on trays in little
paper bags or twists of newspaper. A mandoline
is a useful tool for this dish—you can buy quite
inexpensive plastic Japanese versions as well
as beautiful wooden French ones. Be careful of
your fingers when shaving the vegetables.
You can use the chips as a garnish on other
dishes, such as soup (page 22) or risotto (page 38).

1 lb. green-skinned pumpkin, seeded but not peeled
1 lb. orange sweet potatoes
1 lb. white sweet potatoes
1 large green plantain or 2 green bananas (optional)
sea salt and freshly ground black pepper
sunflower oil, for frying
hot paprika or chili powder, to serve

SERVES 12

Using a vegetable peeler, slice very thin sections off the pumpkin, keeping an
edge of green skin on each if possible. Use a vegetable peeler or mandoline to
slice the remaining vegetables (cut them into strips just wide enough to fit).

Fill a wok or kettle one-third full of the oil or a deep-fryer to the manufacturer's
recommended level. Heat to 375°F or until a cube of bread browns in
30 seconds. Add the vegetable slices in batches and fry until crisp and golden.
Remove with a slotted spoon and drain on crumpled paper towels.

Keep them warm in the oven while you cook the remainder. Skim and reheat
the oil between batches as necessary. When all the chips are cooked, serve
immediately or let cool, then transfer to an airtight container until ready to use.

To serve, sprinkle with sea salt and hot paprika or chili powder.

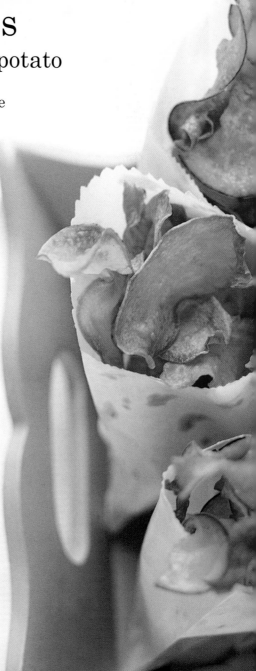

# roasted butternut seeds

Roasted butternut seeds taste a little like pumpkin seeds from health food stores. Both kinds are nice pan-toasted with oil and salt and sprinkled with chili powder.

seeds from 4 or more butternuts, about 2 cups
2–3 tablespoons olive oil
about 1 teaspoon sea salt flakes
crushed dried chiles or chili powder, to taste (optional)

SERVES 2–4 OR MORE

Pull all the fibers away from the seeds. Discard the fibers and put the seeds in a bowl. Sprinkle with olive oil and salt and toss to coat. Spread the seeds over a roasting pan and cook in a preheated oven at 400°F for about 15–20 minutes. Stir after 10 minutes so the seeds are toasted on all sides. Keep checking towards the end of the cooking time—the seeds burn very easily and all ovens vary.

When crisp and toasted, remove from the oven and serve as nibbles, in salads, or on top of pasta or risotto.

# pumpkin samosas

In Mexico, they have empanadas. In England they have Cornish pasties. But in India, they have the samosa, easily the most wonderful of all. Superb street food, it is sold in the bazaars, at railroad stations, and by vendors on street corners. Make half-size samosas to serve as party food. Though not traditional, they are terrific made with puff pastry. I also give the traditional pastry recipe below.

To make the filling, soak the pumpkin and potatoes in cold water for 30 minutes. Cook the peas in boiling salted water until just tender. Drain.

Heat the oil or ghee in a wok or skillet, add the cumin and mustard seeds, and stir-fry until they begin to crackle. Add the ginger and stir-fry for 1 minute. Add the potatoes and chili powder, stir well, cover with a lid, and cook for 2 minutes. Add the pumpkin, stir again, then cook, covered, for 3 minutes. Reduce the heat, cover, and cook until the potatoes are tender. The pumpkin and potatoes should stay in shape and not start to mash. Add the cooked peas and chopped fresh chiles and fry until the mixture is dry. Remove from the heat and let cool. Stir in the chopped cilantro, then divide into 24 portions.

Roll out the pastry to about ⅛-inch thick and cut 4-inch diameter circles with a cookie cutter. Keep the pastry covered with a damp cloth. Cut each disk in half. To fill, put a piece of pastry on your hand, with the straight edge along your forefinger. Brush all the edges with water and overlap the straight sides together to make a cone. Press the edges together. Fill the cone with 1 portion of filling, then press the open edge of the cone together to close. Put on a floured plate and cover with a cloth or plastic, while you make the remainder.

When ready to cook, fill a wok one-third full of the oil or a deep-fryer to the manufacturer's recommended level. Heat to 375°F or when a piece of bread becomes golden brown in 30 seconds. Fry the samosas in batches until puffed and golden, remove with a slotted spoon, and drain on crumpled paper towels. Serve on platters or in baskets as party food, or in paper napkins or paper bags.

14 oz. peeled, seeded orange-fleshed pumpkin or squash, cut into ½-inch cu[
12 oz. potatoes, such as Yukon Gold, cut into ⅛-inch cubes
1½ cups shelled green peas, fresh or frozen
3 tablespoons sunflower oil or ghee
1 teaspoon cumin seeds
1 teaspoon mustard seeds
2 inches fresh ginger, peeled and grated
½–1 teaspoon chili powder
5 red or green chiles, medium or hot, seeded and finely chopped
a large bunch of fresh cilantro, finely chopped
salt
1 package ready-made puff pastry, about 1 lb.
peanut or sunflower oil, for frying

*4-inch cookie cutter*

MAKES 24

## samosa pastry

To make authentic samosa pastry, sift 4 cups all-purpose flour and a pinch of salt into a large bowl. Make a well in the flour and mix in ½ cup peanut or sunflower oil. Gradually add ¾ cup water to make a stiffish dough. Cover with plastic wrap or a damp cloth and chill for 15 minutes. Divide into 12–24 parts, roll into balls and cover with a damp cloth. When ready to fill, roll each ball into a circle, cut in half, fill, moisten the edges of the pastry, then seal and fry as in the main recipe.

# chile pumpkin babycakes

The sweetness of pumpkin is a brilliant marriage partner for spicy chiles. Based on Thai street food, these little morsels make fabulous finger food.

1 cup mashed boiled pumpkin or grated baby zucchinis, about 8 oz.
2 eggs
1 onion, grated
1 garlic clove, crushed
2 green chiles, seeded and finely sliced
green tops of 4 scallions, sliced
2 tablespoons chopped fresh parsley
1 teaspoon salt
½ cup all-purpose flour
1¼ cups unsweetened shredded coconut
cayenne pepper (optional)
sunflower or peanut oil, for frying
soy sauce or chile sauce, to serve

MAKES ABOUT 24

Put the pumpkin or zucchinis in a bowl, add the eggs, onion, garlic, chiles, scallions, parsley, and salt and mix well. Sift the flour into the bowl and mix well. Put the coconut on a plate and sprinkle with the cayenne, if using. Dip a tablespoon in water, then scoop out spoonfuls of the mixture. Using wet hands, roll into balls, then roll them in the coconut until coated.

Heat about 1 inch oil in a non-stick frying pan, add the balls and fry on all sides until crisp and golden. Serve as fingerfood at a party with a dip of soy sauce or chile sauce.

# coconut foogath
## with zucchinis or pumpkin

The foogath is a popular, easy-to-make Indian vegetable dish. Usually made containing shredded cabbage or beans, it can also be made with grated or finely sliced zucchinis, barely cooked, or cubes of pumpkin. In my house, it is a favorite accompaniment for roasted chicken.

2 lb. pumpkin or butternut, peeled and seeded, or 1 lb. baby zucchinis
2–4 tablespoons peanut or mustard oil
1 tablespoon butter or ghee
2 large onions, finely diced
3–6 garlic cloves, crushed
about 1 inch fresh ginger, peeled and grated
1 green chile, seeded and sliced (optional)
4–6 tablespoons unsweetened shredded coconut*

SERVES 4

If using pumpkin or butternut, cut into ½-inch cubes. Par-boil until just tender (about 5 minutes). Drain. If using zucchinis, cut lengthways into 3 pieces and boil or microwave for 2 minutes until *al dente*.

Heat the oil and butter or ghee in a skillet. Add the onion and sauté gently until golden but not browned. Stir in the garlic, ginger and chile, if using, and sauté until the garlic is softened and lightly golden. Add the coconut and pumpkin, butternut, or zucchinis. Sauté for a few minutes—do not let the coconut brown. Serve immediately.

**\*Note:** If preferred, you can soak the coconut in water to cover for about 30 minutes (even overnight). But if the coconut is very fine and good quality, you can use it straight from the package.

# italian pumpkin bean soup

Whatever kind of cabbage you choose for this soup, make sure
you don't cook it any longer than 7–8 minutes. Cabbage doesn't
like it, and will punish you with a dreadful smell. This is also
nice sprinkled with scallions and chopped red chile at the end.

4 red bell peppers, halved and seeded
¼ cup olive oil
4 onions
3 garlic cloves, crushed
3 lb. pumpkin or butternut squash, peeled, seeded, and cut
    into 1-inch cubes or wedges
1½ cups chicken stock
6 oz. cavalo nero or other cabbage, cut into 2-inch pieces
3 cups canned cannellini beans, rinsed and drained
sea salt and freshly ground black pepper
fresh Parmesan cheese, cut in long shavings, to serve
    (optional)

SERVES 4

Put the peppers under a hot broiler, skin side up, and cook until the skins
blacken. Transfer to a small saucepan, cover tightly with a lid, and let stand for
about 5–10 minutes to steam. Remove from the pan and scrape off and discard
the skins. Cut each half into 3 pieces. Set aside.

Heat the oil in a large, heavy-bottom saucepan. Add the onions and sauté gently
until softened and translucent. Add the garlic and sauté until golden. Add the
pumpkin and toss until well covered with the flavored oil and lightly browned.

Add the stock and bring to a boil. Add the cavolo nero or cabbage and the
reserved peppers, return to a boil, then simmer for about 6 minutes. Stir in
the beans, add salt and pepper to taste, heat until bubbling, then serve sprinkled
with shavings of fresh Parmesan.

# japanese squash and miso soup

My nephew is a professional potter and, like many potters, bananas about Japan. I have him to thank for this delicious and unusual soup. Dried seaweed is a delicious addition to this soup too. Use Japanese kabocha squash or ordinary butternuts.

6 cups stock (dashi if possible, otherwise vegetable or chicken)
8 inches daikon (white radish or mooli), peeled and diced
1 lb. kabocha or butternut squash or pumpkin, peeled, seeded, and cut into ½-inch cubes
1 block fresh tofu, about 8 oz., cut into ½-inch cubes
1 leek or 2 shallots, sliced
1 inch fresh ginger, peeled and grated
3 garlic cloves, crushed
1 cup fresh corn kernels (from 2 fresh cobs)
6 shiitake mushrooms, halved or sliced
1 head broccoli, broken into small florets
2 oz. instant miso powder
12 scallions, sliced

SERVES 4

Put the stock in a large saucepan and bring to a boil. Add the daikon, squash or pumpkin, tofu, leek or shallots, ginger, and garlic. Return to a boil, reduce the heat, and simmer for 15 minutes. Add the corn, mushrooms, and broccoli and simmer for 5 minutes.

Put the miso in a large measuring cup, add 1 cup liquid from the pan, and stir until dissolved. Remove the soup from the heat, stir in the miso and scallions, then serve.

# pumpkin soup

Many people prefer this classic French soup made without potatoes, but I find that they thicken the soup nicely and smooth the strong, very sweet taste of pumpkin. The milk is important—pumpkin loves milk—and it's also very fond of nutmeg.

Put the pumpkin and potatoes in a large saucepan, add chicken stock or boiling water to cover, then simmer until tender. Drain, reserving the cooking liquid.

Heat the butter and oil in a skillet, add the onions, and sauté until softened and lightly golden. Transfer to a blender or food processor, then add the pumpkin and potatoes, in batches if necessary. Blend, adding enough milk and cooking liquid to make a thick purée.

Transfer the purée to the saucepan and stir in enough stock to make a thick, creamy soup. Add salt to taste, reheat without boiling, then ladle into heated soup bowls. Top with sour cream, nutmeg, and a few pumpkin chips.

2 lb. pumpkin, preferably green or gray-skinned, peeled, seeded and cut into large chunks
2 large potatoes, quartered
4 cups boiling chicken stock
4 tablespoons unsalted butter
2 tablespoons olive oil
2 large onions, finely sliced
1 cup milk
sea salt

**TO SERVE:**
4 tablespoons sour cream
freshly grated nutmeg
pumpkin chips (page 16)

SERVES 4

---

### roasted pumpkin soup
Roast the pumpkin instead of boiling it, to give a smoky taste.

### pumpkin, ginger, and coconut soup
Substitute coconut milk for the fresh milk and include 1 inch fresh ginger, sliced, and 2 crushed garlic cloves with the vegetables before boiling. Omit the nutmeg and serve sprinkled with torn fresh cilantro leaves.

# vegetable dishes

# pumpkin and pepper kabobs
## marinated in ginger oil

For this dish, try to find pumpkins with gray, blue-gray, or green skins—most common in Asian stores or Caribbean markets. This type has a good, firm texture, suitable for skewering, plus wonderful taste and brilliant color. Butternut squash is also delicious, but softer, so par-boil or microwave it for a shorter time.

½ cup olive oil
1 inch fresh ginger, peeled and grated
2 orange or red bell peppers, halved and seeded
1 lb. peeled and seeded firm-fleshed pumpkin
1 lb. peeled orange sweet potato
sea salt and freshly ground black pepper

*about 8 metal or bamboo skewers (if bamboo, soak in water for 30 minutes)*

SERVES 4

Heat the olive oil and ginger in a small saucepan and set aside to steep.

Broil the pepper halves until the skin blisters, then put in a saucepan and cover tightly. Let steam for 10 minutes, then scrape off the skin. Cut the peppers into 1-inch squares.

Meanwhile, cut the pumpkin into 1-inch cubes and par-boil or microwave until half-cooked. Drain, then thread the pumpkin and pepper alternately onto the skewers. Put on a shallow dish and brush thickly with the ginger oil. Set aside until ready to cook.

When ready to cook, turn the skewers to cover the vegetables with the ginger oil again, sprinkle with salt and pepper, then cook on a grill or under a broiler for about 15 minutes until cooked through and browned at the edges. Test for tenderness, cook for 5 minutes longer if necessary, then serve.

# roasted pumpkin
## with other vegetables

Every Australian and New Zealander grows up with pumpkin served with the
Sunday roast as a matter of course. Roasted potatoes, roasted pumpkin, and
whatever your mother fancied as a green vegetable (you prayed she wouldn't
decide on peas, because you knew who would have to shell them). Some people
don't peel the pumpkin, but I always do because I love all the toasted edges.

½ green or gray-skinned pumpkin
6 medium baking potatoes, peeled and halved lengthwise
2 red bell peppers, halved lengthwise and seeded
4 red onions, quartered lengthwise through the root
  (root intact)
2 large orange-fleshed sweet potatoes, peeled, halved
  crosswise, then lengthwise
4 bay leaves
4 sprigs of fresh thyme or rosemary
8 garlic cloves, unpeeled but lightly crushed with a fork
olive oil, for frying
sea salt and freshly ground black pepper

SERVES 4

Seed the pumpkin—use an ice-cream scoop and remove all the fibers. If you're
going to peel the pumpkin, put it cut side down on a chopping board and slice off
the skin patiently and in small sections. Use a sharp knife and don't hurry. Cut the
pumpkin into wedges (cut each wedge in half crosswise if preferred).  You can also
peel them after cutting into wedges, which can be easier.

Put the potatoes into a plastic bag, add olive oil, salt, and lots of freshly ground
black pepper. Toss until well coated. Repeat with the peppers and onion wedges.

Brush a heavy-based roasting pan with olive oil and heat it on top of the stove. Add
the onions and potatoes, curved side down, and the peppers, cut side up. Roast in
a preheated oven at 400°F for about 20 minutes.

Add the pumpkin and sweet potatoes to the plastic bag, add more olive oil if
necessary, and toss as before. Add to the roasting pan and turn the other vegetables
over at the same time. Tuck the bay leaves, thyme or rosemary, and garlic cloves
around the vegetables and return the pan to the oven. Cook for another 20 minutes.

Test that all the vegetables are done, then serve with roasted meats or—for
vegetarians—beans or chickpeas.

# jamaican curry
## with zucchinis, pattypans, and pumpkin

Vary the vegetables in this curry depending on what's good in the market, as a local cook would in Jamaica. Gray- or green-skinned pumpkin is used in the Caribbean, but you can also make this dish with orange-skinned butternut squash. Just remember it won't need quite as long to cook—the flesh is a little softer than pumpkin. If you leave out the bacon, this curry is a spicy treat for vegetarians.

2 tablespoons sunflower or peanut oil
4 oz. bacon or pancetta, snipped into strips (optional)
½ Scotch bonnet chile, seeded and sliced
½ teaspoon allspice berries, crushed
½ teaspoon freshly grated nutmeg
6 green cardamom pods, crushed
1 red onion, cut into wedges through the root
2 cups chicken stock
2 cups unsweetened coconut milk
boiled rice, to serve

**YOUR CHOICE OF AT LEAST 5 OF THE FOLLOWING:**
8 oz. pumpkin chunks
2 orange-fleshed sweet potatoes, cut into chunks
1 plantain or green banana, peeled and thickly sliced diagonally
1 chayote (chow-chow, mirliton, christophine, or choko), diced
8 round yellow or white eggplants or small purple ones
8 pattypan squash or 4 baby zucchinis
1 cup sugarsnap peas
2 large red bell peppers, halved, or 6 mini peppers, charred, peeled, and seeded

SERVES 4

Heat half the sunflower or peanut oil in a skillet, add the bacon or pancetta, if using, and cook until crisp. Remove and drain on paper towels. Add the remaining oil to the skillet, add the chile, allspice, nutmeg, and cardamom and stir-fry for about 2 minutes to release the aromatic oils.

Add the onion wedges and cook until softened and slightly browned. Turn and cook the other side. Remove and set aside.

Add your choice of the pumpkin, sweet potatoes, plantain or banana, chayote, and eggplants and turn until well coated with the spices. Add the stock and cook until almost done.

Add the pattypans or zucchinis, and cook for 2 minutes. Add the sugarsnaps, pour in the coconut milk, and bring to just below boiling (take care or the milk will split). Add the prepared red peppers and reserved onions, reheat gently, then remove from the heat.

Transfer to a large serving bowl, top with crispy bacon, if using, and serve with boiled rice. To serve a larger number of guests, add a meat or chicken curry—to stay with the Caribbean theme, make it goat, pork, or chicken.

# moroccan vegetable tagine
## with pumpkin, pattypans, and zucchinis

Tagines are the conical-lidded terracotta cooking pots of Morocco, and also the dishes cooked in them. Any large covered casserole can be used for this recipe—a modern version of the classic *Couscous aux Sept Légumes*. Use any number of vegetables, and serve alone or with a chicken tagine.

Put the couscous in a heatproof bowl, add enough boiling stock to cover by about 1 inch. Stir in the harissa paste and set aside while you prepare the vegetables. Cover and keep warm in the oven.

Heat the olive oil in a skillet and sauté the onions until soft. Add the garlic, cardamom and coriander seeds, and cinnamon and stir-fry until the garlic is golden. Add the pumpkin, carrots, salt, pepper, and 1 cup boiling chicken stock, cover, and cook for 10 minutes more. Add the zucchinis, pattypans, and chickpeas, cover and cook for 5 minutes.

Add extra boiling chicken stock if necessary to make about ½-inch depth of liquid in the skillet, then add the sugarsnaps or green beans, return to a boil, replace the lid for about 30 seconds, then serve immediately. Fluff up the couscous with a fork and transfer to a serving plate. Top with the vegetable mixture and lots of chopped fresh cilantro.

---

### chicken tagine

This vegetable couscous dish is also wonderful served with a traditional chicken tagine. Heat 3 tablespoons olive oil in a flameproof casserole, add a whole chicken, and brown on all sides. Add 2 grated onions, a large pinch of saffron strands, 2 crushed garlic cloves, 1 teaspoon cardamom pods, crushed, 2 broken cinnamon sticks, salt, pepper, and 1 cup water. Bring to a boil, cover with a lid, and simmer for about 1–1½ hours, or until very tender.

---

2½ cups quick-cook couscous
3 cups boiling chicken or vegetable stock
2 tablespoons harissa paste
2 tablespoons olive oil
2 onions, sliced
4 garlic cloves (to taste), crushed
black seeds from 6 green cardamom pods, crushed
1 teaspoon crushed coriander seeds
1 cinnamon stick, broken
4 oz. pumpkin, cut into 1-inch cubes
4 oz. baby carrots, whole
4 oz. baby zucchinis, green and yellow, halved lengthwise
4 oz. baby pattypan squash, halved crosswise
about 1 cup cooked chickpeas, or canned and drained
1 cup sugarsnap peas or small green beans
salt and freshly ground black pepper
a large bunch of fresh cilantro, coarsely chopped

SERVES 4

# pumpkin gnocchi

Microwaving pumpkin keeps its flesh dry, so the gnocchi won't be too sloppy. However, you'll have better color if you boil it, then let steam dry. Gnocchi are usually made by flipping balls of dough off the end of a fork. I prefer this simpler method, taught to me by friend and fellow food writer Alastair Hendy. I think they look like little pillows.

2 lb. pumpkin flesh, cubed (choose a dense-fleshed variety)
3 egg yolks
1 teaspoon salt
1–1¼ cups all-purpose flour, sifted
leaves from a large bunch of flat-leaf parsley, chopped
semolina, for dusting

**TO SERVE:**
shavings of Parmesan cheese
deep-fried parsley or sage leaves (optional)*
olive oil
freshly cracked black pepper

SERVES 4

Cook the pumpkin in boiling salted water until just tender. Drain and let steam dry in the strainer. Mash or press through a potato ricer into a bowl. Add the egg yolks, salt, flour, and parsley and work to a firm dough, adding more flour if necessary. Divide the dough into 4 pieces and roll each piece into a long cylinder, about 1 inch thick. Cut each cylinder into 1-inch segments, like little pillows, then put on a board or plate sprinkled with semolina.

Bring a large saucepan of water to a boil, add the gnocchi in batches, and cook for 3–4 minutes each batch or until they float to the top of the pan. Drain, then serve in heated plates topped with the Parmesan, fried leaves, and olive oil. Sprinkle with pepper and serve.

**\*Note:** To fry parsley or sage leaves, put 2 tablespoons oil in a small skillet and heat until very hot. Add the leaves, fry for a few seconds until crisp, then drain on crumpled paper towels.

# pumpkin risotto

A Pacific-Rim version of *Risotto al Zucca*.
Pumpkin is a much-loved vegetable in New
Zealand and Australia—roasted, puréed, or
souped. This is a variation on those cooking
methods. The potatoes are optional, but if
you use a butternut squash, they will help
compensate for its looser texture.

Put the pumpkin or butternut and potatoes in a saucepan, barely cover with
water, add salt, and simmer until the vegetables are tender. Drain, reserving the
cooking water. Purée the pumpkin and potatoes with half the butter (I use an
immersion blender), and add enough of the cooking water to make a thick,
soupy mixture—add a little milk if necessary. Keep the mixture hot.

Heat the oil and remaining butter in a skillet, add the onions, and sauté gently
until soft and translucent. Add the garlic and cook until lightly golden, about
1–2 minutes. Add the rice and stir-fry for 1–2 minutes until the grains are
well covered with oil. Add a quarter of the boiling stock and simmer gently,
stirring, until absorbed.

Repeat until all the stock has been used and the risotto is creamy and fluffy,
about 18–20 minutes. Stir the reserved pumpkin purée through the risotto and
serve, topped with the Parmesan, pumpkin chips, and herbs, if using.

1 lb. peeled and seeded pumpkin or butternut squash
4 potatoes, peeled and cut into large chunks (optional)
2 tablespoons butter
milk (optional—see method)
¼ cup olive oil
2 onions, finely chopped
2 fat garlic cloves, crushed
2 cups risotto rice, such as arborio or carnaroli
4 cups boiling chicken stock
salt

**TO SERVE:**
Your choice of:
shavings of Parmesan cheese
pumpkin chips (page 16)
sprigs of chervil or deep-fried
    sliced sage leaves (page 37)

SERVES 4

# butternut and zucchini pulao

Pulaos were born in Persia, but versions are found all the way from India to the Middle East and Spain. The name changes from pulao to pullaw, pilaf and then paella along the way. Use wonderful, scented basmati rice from the foothills of the Himalaya for this dish and remember, rice is always measured by volume, not by weight. I make this without cumin seeds, though they are traditional.

a pinch of saffron strands or ½ teaspoon turmeric*
½ cup sunflower oil
2 cloves, crushed
1 teaspoon cumin seeds
1 onion, finely sliced
1 tablespoon green cardamom pods, crushed
1 cinnamon stick, broken
2 bay leaves
½ cauliflower head, separated into florets
½ butternut squash, peeled, seeded and cut into ½-inch cubes
2 potatoes, cut into ½-inch cubes
1 cup shelled green peas, fresh or frozen
1 carrot, cut into small cubes
2 cups basmati rice, washed and drained
1 inch fresh ginger, peeled and grated
a pinch of sugar
4 zucchinis, cut into 1-inch chunks

**TO SERVE:**
⅔ cup cashews
⅔ cup shelled pistachios
a large handful of cilantro leaves (optional)

SERVES 6

Put the saffron strands, if using, into a teacup, cover with boiling water and let infuse for as long as possible, or until the rice is done.

Heat ⅓ cup of the sunflower oil in a large, heavy-bottom saucepan. Add the cloves and cumin seeds and sauté for about 10 seconds. Add the sliced onions and stir-fry until softened and translucent. Add the cardamom, cinnamon, bay leaves, cauliflower, butternut, potatoes, peas, and carrot. Stir-fry until covered with oil, then cover with a lid, lower the heat and simmer for 5 minutes. Stir in the rice, add 4 cups water, the ginger, and sugar. Bring to a boil, cover with a lid, reduce the heat and simmer until all the water has been absorbed and the rice is fluffy, about 10–12 minutes. Do not lift the lid, or you will spoil it.

Meanwhile, heat the remaining oil in a small skillet, add the zucchinis, and stir-fry for 1–2 minutes at a high heat until lightly browned but still firm. Set aside.

Turn out the rice onto a serving dish, add the zucchinis, then sprinkle with the cashews, pistachios, and cilantro. Carefully drizzle over the saffron liquid to make yellow trails in the rice. Serve.

**\*Note:** If using turmeric, add it at the same time as the onions.

# entrées

# baked whole stuffed pumpkin

My sister grows what in my opinion is the best pumpkin of all—the Queensland Blue. It is a squashed turban shape, with a beautiful dark blue-green-gray skin and brilliant orange flesh. It is very dense and firm. She cooks this in the oven, or in a kettle-style barbecue. Choose one large pumpkin or several smaller ones.

Using a small, sharp knife, cut a "plug" out of the top of the pumpkin, including the stalk, if any, and reserve. Using an ice cream scoop or metal spoon, scoop out and discard all the seeds and fibers. Brush the inside of the pumpkin with olive oil.

Par-boil the carrots in boiling salted water until almost cooked. Drain and set aside.

Put 1 tablespoon olive oil in a non-stick skillet, add the bacon, and stir-fry until crisp. Remove with a slotted spoon and drain on crumpled paper towels.

Add the onions to the skillet and sauté until softened and translucent. Add the garlic and ginger and stir-fry until the onion is golden. Add the oregano or thyme and the beef and stir-fry until the meat is browned. Stir in the tomato purée and chiles. Add the carrots, bacon, and rice and stir-fry until hot—the mixture should be fairly stiff.

Mix in the parsley then use the mixture to stuff the pumpkin—the mixture is already cooked, so it won't expand. Put the lid on top and wrap in a "basin" of foil. Bake in a preheated oven at 400°F for 45–60 minutes or until the pumpkin is tender. Test with the point of a skewer—the time will depend on the pumpkin variety and its size.

**Variation:** Wrap in foil and cook in a kettle-style barbecue for 45 minutes or until tender as above. Serve in wedges with salad leaves dressed with pumpkin oil.

1 large pumpkin, about 6 lb., or 6 small pumpkins
olive oil, for brushing

**FILLING:**
1–2 carrots, sliced
2 tablespoons olive oil
4 slices bacon, chopped
1–2 onions, finely sliced
3 garlic cloves, crushed
1 inch fresh ginger, peeled and finely chopped
leaves from 3–4 sprigs of oregano or thyme, chopped
2 cups ground beef
2 teaspoons tomato purée
1–2 fresh red chiles, halved, seeded, and chopped
1 cup cooked white rice
leaves from 1 large bunch of flat-leaf parsley, chopped
sea salt and freshly ground black pepper

SERVES 6–8

# pumpkin soufflé

In spite of their fearsome reputation, soufflés are easy to make and a perfect lunch for two. You just have to have everyone ready and waiting to eat. The top should be browned and the inside light and creamy—a dish with its sauce all in one recipe. Each person should get some browned crusty outsides and creamy insides.

1 lb. peeled and seeded pumpkin
a pinch of salt
2 tablespoons unsalted butter
3 tablespoons all-purpose flour
⅔ cup milk
3 eggs, separated, plus 2 extra egg whites
1 cup grated Gruyère cheese
1 tablespoon grated Parmesan cheese
a pinch of freshly grated nutmeg
sea salt and freshly ground black pepper

**FOR THE SOUFFLÉ DISH:**
butter, for greasing
1 tablespoon Parmesan cheese

*1 soufflé dish, 5 cups, or 6 small ramekins*
*kitchen twine and buttered waxed paper*

SERVES 2–3 AS AN ENTRÉE, 4–6 AS AN APPETIZER

Lightly grease the soufflé dish with butter, then add 1 tablespoon of the Parmesan and shake it around until well coated. If you use a small ramekin, tie a tube of waxed paper around it with kitchen twine. If using a larger one, you won't have to.

Cut the pumpkin into 1-inch chunks, put in a saucepan with a pinch of salt, add 1 cup boiling water, bring to a boil, and simmer until tender. Drain, let steam dry in the strainer for a few minutes, then purée in a food processor or blender, or with an immersion blender. Set aside until almost cool.

Melt the butter in a saucepan, add the flour, and stir in well with a wire whisk. Cook for 30–60 seconds to burst the starch grains. Beat in the hot milk, and keep beating until the mixture thickens to form a thick white sauce. Alternatively, put the butter, flour, and milk in a saucepan and beat over a moderate heat until thickened. Season with salt and pepper. Mix in the pumpkin purée and the egg yolks, one at a time. Stir in the two cheeses and the nutmeg. Return to the heat for a moment, stir several times, then transfer to a bowl.

Put the 5 egg whites into a very clean, grease-free bowl. Using an equally grease-free balloon whisk or electric beater, beat until soft peaks form. Using a metal spoon, cut 1 tablespoon of egg whites into the pumpkin mixture. Add one-third of the egg whites and fold through lightly with the same spoon. Add the remaining egg whites and fold gently through, keeping as much air in the mixture as possible. Do not stir, or you will lose all the air and the soufflé will not rise.

Pour the soufflé mixture into the prepared soufflé dish or dishes. Run your finger around the edge of the mixture to help it rise away from the edges. Cook in a preheated oven at 400°F for about 30 minutes for a large soufflé or 15–18 minutes if small. The soufflé should have risen well, be brown on the top, and soft and creamy in the middle. Take to the table immediately and serve.

# spicy butternut curry

## with chicken and spinach

This is a variation on an easy but marvelous curry recipe taught to me by a friend. It is beautifully orange, just like her cat. I don't think they would recognize this dish in India, but I am sure they'd love it.

2 tablespoons sunflower or peanut oil
1 tablespoon mustard seeds
1 lb. butternut or pumpkin, peeled, seeded, and cut into 1-inch cubes
2 onions, finely sliced
2 garlic cloves, crushed
1 inch fresh ginger, peeled and grated (optional)
a pinch of ground turmeric
4 chicken breasts, skinless and boneless, cut into 1-inch slices
1 lb. tomatoes, peeled and coarsely chopped
1 cup heavy cream
1 large package of spinach, about 1 lb.
a pinch of ground cumin or garam masala (from Indian stores)
sea salt and freshly ground black pepper

SERVES 4

Heat the oil in a non-stick skillet or wok, add the mustard seeds, and stir-fry until they pop. Add half the butternut or pumpkin and all of the onions and stir-fry gently until the onions are softened and translucent. Add the garlic, ginger, salt, and pepper and stir-fry for 1 minute. Add the turmeric and stir-fry for 1 minute more.

Add the chicken, stir-fry until sealed on all sides, then add the tomatoes and remaining butternut or pumpkin. Bring to a boil, then reduce the heat, and simmer, covered, for about 20 minutes, or until tender.

Add the cream, bring to a boil, and simmer, stirring, until thickened—the cream will first boil with large bubbles, then small. Stop at this point or the cream will curdle. Add the spinach and cumin or garam masala, cover with a lid, and steam for 2 minutes until the leaves collapse, then stir into the rest of the ingredients. Serve with steamed basmati rice and other curry dishes or with naan bread.

# vietnamese chicken curry
## with pumpkin and coconut milk

Our family loves Vietnamese food, because it tastes fresher than Chinese food. This recipe is easy and delicious.

1 tablespoon peanut oil
2 stalks of lemongrass, peeled and lower section finely sliced
1 onion, finely sliced
2–3 garlic cloves, crushed
1 inch fresh ginger, peeled and finely sliced
3 red chiles, finely sliced (seeded if preferred)
6 boneless, skinless chicken breasts, sliced crosswise into 3 pieces each
12 baby carrots, trimmed
8 oz. peeled and seeded pumpkin, cut into 1-inch pieces
½ cup canned unsweetened coconut milk
2 tablespoons fish sauce
1 teaspoon sugar
6 scallions, halved and finely sliced lengthwise
sprigs of cilantro, to serve

SERVES 4

Heat the oil in a wok, add the lemongrass, onion, garlic, and ginger and stir-fry for 2–3 minutes or until the onion is softened and translucent. Add 2 of the chiles and the chicken and stir-fry until golden.

Add 2 cups water, bring to a boil, reduce the heat, and simmer for 30 minutes. Add the carrots, pumpkin, and coconut milk and simmer, uncovered, until the pumpkin is tender and the chicken cooked through.

Stir in the fish sauce and sugar, sprinkle with scallions, the remaining chile, and the sprigs of cilantro and serve with fragrant Thai rice.

# stuffed sugar pumpkins
## with pesto and goat cheese

Choose small sugar pumpkins or butternut squash for this recipe (or just the bottom half and use the top piece for other recipes). This is marvelous served with salad as an entrée vegetarian lunch. If the butternuts are large, you may find one between two people is right.

4 small sugar pumpkins or butternut squash, washed
   and dried
2 small red onions, diced
16–20 cherry tomatoes, halved
a large handful of basil leaves
4 tablespoons pesto
2 small goat cheeses or mozzarella, torn into pieces
olive oil, for brushing
sea salt and freshly ground black pepper

SERVES 4

If using sugar pumpkins, cut off a "lid" and reserve. Scoop out the centers with an ice cream scoop to make smooth. If using butternuts, cut them off just as they start to narrow into a "waist" and scoop out the seeds—you're aiming for a hollow receptacle. (Use the tops of the butternuts for another dish.)

Put the onions in a strainer set over a bowl and cover with boiling water. Leave for about 2 minutes, then drain, pat dry with paper towels, and distribute among the pumpkins. Add the tomato halves, the basil leaves, a generous tablespoon or two of pesto, then the goat cheeses or mozzarella. Sprinkle with sea salt and freshly ground black pepper. The hollows should be nicely filled with the ingredients.

Brush the pumpkins all over with olive oil, brushing the top of the cheese. Set the "lids", if any, slightly askew. Arrange in an oiled baking tray or dish and cook in a preheated oven at 400°F until tender. Test with a metal skewer after 20 minutes, then every 5–10 minutes until done (the time will depend on the size of your pumpkins).

Serve with a crisp, peppery salad.

# pumpkin griddle cakes

My Grannie was a redoubtable Scotswoman and, like all Scots, an inspired baker. A griddle is a kind of skillet—quite flat, and with a bucket-style handle—used before ovens were common in domestic kitchens. The finished griddle cakes were stacked up against the handle to dry out a little before serving. Grannie was always covered in clouds of flour when making these cakes. Nostalgia!

3½ cups all-purpose flour
1 cup cooked mashed pumpkin, quite dry
½ teaspoon salt
¼ teaspoon baking soda
1 tablespoon unsalted butter, melted
¾ cup buttermilk
3 tablespoons mild molasses
suet, shortening, or sunflower oil, for brushing

MAKES 8

Sift the flour into a large bowl and mix in the pumpkin, salt, baking soda, butter, buttermilk, and molasses. Bring the mixture together to form a soft dough, then transfer to a floured surface. Pat out to a slab about ½ inch thick—don't handle it too much or the griddle cakes will be tough. Trim the edges. Cut into 4 squares, then each square into 2 triangles.

Heat a large griddle or cast-iron skillet and, when hot, rub it all over with a piece of suet or shortening or brush with oil. Cook the griddle cakes, in batches, for about 3–4 minutes, turning halfway through cooking time until browned. Stack against the handle to let dry out a little before serving.

Alternatively, bake in a preheated oven at 400°F for 15–20 minutes. Serve with your choice of butter, jelly, whipped cream—and lots of tea or coffee.

# farmhouse pumpkin biscuits

These biscuits are a great tradition where I come from. Any housewife worth her salt can turn them out by the shedload at the drop of a hat. Children took them to school for lunch, spread with butter and jam or Vegemite—a particularly Australian concoction that horrifies anyone from any other part of the world. My mother never used a cookie cutter to cut them out, but you get pretty shapes if you do.

1 tablespoon unsalted butter, softened
6 tablespoons sugar
1 egg, lightly beaten
1 cup cooked mashed pumpkin*
2¼ cups self-rising flour, sifted
a pinch of salt
extra beaten egg or milk, to glaze

*a 2½-inch plain or fluted cookie cutter*
*a baking tray, lightly greased*

MAKES 8 ROUND BISCUITS OR 12 CUT-OUT BISCUITS

Using an electric beater, cream the butter and sugar in a bowl, then beat in the egg, a little at a time. Beat in the mashed pumpkin, then stir in the flour and salt with a wooden spoon. Bring the mixture together to form a soft but not sticky dough. If it seems dry and won't come together, add 1–2 tablespoons milk.

Transfer to a floured work surface and pat out to about ¾ inch thick. Cut into 8 squares and pat each square into a ball. Alternatively, using a cookie cutter, stamp out rounds. Gather trimmings, pat out again, and cut out more rounds—don't handle too much, or the biscuits will become tough.

Arrange the biscuits apart on the prepared baking tray and brush with beaten egg or milk. Bake in a preheated oven at 350°F for about 15 minutes, then remove from the oven and transfer to a wire rack to cool.

**\*Note:** In this recipe, as in all baking, it is important to use a dry-fleshed mealy pumpkin—other varieties are too wet, and you have to add extra flour. Find these varieties in Asian, African, or Caribbean markets—you'll know them by their green, gray, or gray-green skins. The Japanese kabocha is also suitable.

# pumpkin cake

This cake is filled with fruit goodies and sweet pumpkin. Use as many interesting dried fruits as you can find—the original recipe, like the zucchini bread on page 62—comes from East Africa. I use mango, papaya, candied cherries, and citrus peel, but be creative.

2½ cups mixed dried fruit
⅓ cup candied cherries, halved
½ cup mixed peel
1⅔ cups sugar
1 tablespoon golden syrup or corn syrup
½ cup (1 stick) butter
1 level teaspoon baking soda
2 eggs, lightly beaten
8 oz. cooked mashed pumpkin, very dry
¾ cup all-purpose flour
1 cup plus 3 tablespoons self-rising flour

*one 9-inch round springform cake pan, greased and lined with a double layer of waxed paper*

MAKES ONE 9-INCH CAKE

Put the mixed fruit, cherries, peel, sugar, golden syrup or corn syrup, butter, baking soda, and 1 cup cold water in a saucepan. Bring to a boil, then simmer for 20 minutes. Let cool.

Transfer the cooled fruit mixture to a mixing bowl. Add the beaten eggs and mashed pumpkin and beat until smooth. Sift the flours together, then stir into the mixture. Spoon the mixture into the prepared cake pan and bake in a preheated oven at 350°F for 1 hour, then reduce the temperature to 300°F and bake for 1–1½ hours until a skewer inserted into the center of the cake comes out clean. Remove from the oven and cool on a wire rack.

# pumpkin pie

A friend of mine, who hails from New Hampshire, is the doyenne of pumpkin pie makers. She is marooned in Australia, far from a proper can of pumpkin purée, so she has to make it from fresh pumpkin. The maple syrup is her secret ingredient.

2 pie crusts, 8 inches diameter, or 1 lb. ready-made shortcrust pastry
whipped cream or ice cream, to serve

**PUMPKIN FILLING:**
3 eggs
1 lb. canned solid-pack pumpkin or 2 cups cooked puréed pumpkin
1 cup plus 3 tablespoons sugar
½ cup maple syrup
¼ teaspoon salt
⅛ teaspoon freshly grated nutmeg
⅛ teaspoon ground cloves
⅛ teaspoon ground ginger
½–1 teaspoon ground cinnamon
1⅔ cups evaporated milk

*2 pies dishes or removable-bottom tart pans, 8-inch diameter, greased*

MAKES 2 PIES, 8 INCHES DIAMETER

If using ready-made shortcrust pastry, put on a floured surface and roll to about ⅛ inch thick. Use to line the dishes or pans, crimping the edges decoratively. Line with waxed paper and dried beans or rice. Bake in a preheated oven at 375°F for 12–15 minutes, then remove the beans and paper and bake for a further 5 minutes.

Put the remaining ingredients in a bowl and beat with an electric beater at high speed for 5 minutes. Pour into the pie shells, then cook in the middle of a preheated oven at 350°F for 45 minutes. Cool, then serve with cream or ice cream. Store in the refrigerator if making the day before, then reheat—it should not be served cold.

# pumpkin curd tartlets

Lemon curd is one of my favorite teatime treats—wonderful in tartlets, in larger tarts, and even on toast. Pumpkin curd is sweeter and very delicious and the extra spice makes it even better. You should use the dense-fleshed green or gray-skinned pumpkin for this recipe.

2 lb. pumpkin, halved, seeded, peeled, and cut into
    1½-inch chunks (to make 2 cups purée)
2 inches fresh ginger, peeled and grated
grated zest and juice of 1 lime
2 cups preserving sugar
¾ cup (1½ sticks) unsalted butter, cut into cubes
4 eggs, beaten

**TARTLET SHELLS:**
1⅓ cups all-purpose flour
1 teaspoon salt
¼ teaspoon sugar
7 tablespoons unsalted butter, chilled and diced,
1 egg
1 tablespoon milk
confectioners' sugar, for dusting (optional)

*2-inch cookie cutter*
*12-cup, deep muffin pan, greased*

MAKES ABOUT 3 CUPS (3 JARS), 36 TARTLETS

To make the curd, put the pumpkin in a saucepan, add 1 cup water, bring to a boil, reduce the heat, and simmer until tender. Drain, reserving the liquid. Purée the solids in a blender, adding enough liquid to make the blades run.

Squeeze the grated ginger and reserve the juice. Discard the solids. Put the lime zest and juice, ginger juice, pumpkin purée, and sugar in a medium saucepan. Stir over a gentle heat until the sugar dissolves. Strain into a heatproof bowl set over a saucepan of barely simmering water. Add the butter and stir until melted.

Strain the beaten eggs through a fine strainer into the bowl and stir well. Cook gently, stirring often at the beginning, then continuously at the end until the mixture coats the back of a spoon, about 30 minutes. Do not let boil or the mixture will curdle. Remove from the heat and pour into warm sterilized preserving jars. Seal and let cool. Use immediately or store in the refrigerator for up to 1 week.

To make the tartlet shells, put the flour, salt, and sugar in a food processor and pulse to mix. Add the butter and pulse until the mixture resembles fine crumbs. Put the egg and milk into a small bowl and beat with a fork. Add to the food processor and pulse a few times, then process until the dough forms a ball. Wrap in plastic and chill for 30 minutes or up to 1 week. Knead the chilled pastry briefly to soften, then roll out on a lightly floured surface to about ⅛ inch thick. Cut into rounds with the cookie cutter, then use to line the muffin pan. Prick the bases with a fork and cover the remaining pastry with plastic wrap. Bake in a preheated oven at 375°F for about 15 minutes until lightly golden. Remove from the oven, cool in the pan for a few minutes, then transfer to a wire rack to cool completely. Wipe the pan clean and repeat with the remaining pastry.

When ready to serve, fill each tartlet with a large spoon of pumpkin curd, dust with confectioners' sugar, if using, and serve. Leftover curd is marvelous spread on toast for breakfast.

# pumpkin raisin bread

A sweet golden bread that's beautiful plain or buttered —but if you can't get too much of a good thing, spread with strawberry conserve and crème fraîche. Lots of hot green tea or strong caffè latte are also required.

Sift the flour and salt into a large bowl, stir in the dried yeast,* and rub in the butter. Add the mashed pumpkin, cream, raisins, and ¼ cup lukewarm water. Mix to form a soft but not sticky dough. If the dough is too sticky, add more flour, 1 tablespoon at a time, if too dry, more lukewarm water, 1 tablespoon at a time.

Turn out the dough onto a floured surface and knead thoroughly for 10 minutes until smooth and elastic. Return to the bowl and cover. Let rise at normal room temperature until doubled in size—about 1–1½ hours.

Punch down the risen dough. Turn out onto a floured surface and knead briefly. Shape into a loaf and press neatly into the prepared pan. Cover and let rise as before until doubled in size—about 45 minutes.

Brush the risen loaf with beaten egg, then bake in a preheated oven at 400°F for 25 minutes. Reduce to 350°F and bake for a further 15–20 minutes or until the turned-out loaf sounds hollow when tapped underneath. Cool on a wire rack.

*If using fresh yeast, crumble ¾ cake (½ oz.) into a pitcher, add the lukewarm water, and stir until blended. Add to the dry ingredients at the same time as the pumpkin. Proceed as in the main recipe.*

2 cups white bread flour
½ teaspoon salt
2½ teaspoons active dry yeast*
5 tablespoons unsalted butter
7 oz. cooked mashed pumpkin, about 1 cup
½ cup heavy cream, heated
½ cup raisins
1 egg, beaten, to glaze

*one loaf pan, 9 x 5 x 3 inches, greased*

MAKES 1 LARGE LOAF

## zucchini and pecan teabread

Put 3 eggs, 1¼ cups sunflower oil, and 1½ cups sugar in a bowl and beat well until thick. Fold in 1 cup small, green, grated zucchinis. Put 2 cups all-purpose flour into a bowl and mix in 2 teaspoons baking soda, 1 teaspoon baking powder, 1 teaspoon salt, and 2 teaspoons apple pie spice. Stir into the zucchini mixture and fold in ¾ cup chopped pecans. Stir in ½ cup golden raisins or raisins, then transfer to a greased and lined 8-inch cake pan. Bake in a preheated oven at 350°F for 1 hour 15 minutes until well-risen and golden brown, or when a skewer inserted in the middle comes out clean. Remove from the oven, turn out of the pan, and let cool on a wire rack.

# index

# conversion charts

Weights and measures have been rounded up
or down slightly to make measuring easier.

VOLUME EQUIVALENTS:

| American | Metric | Imperial |
| --- | --- | --- |
| 1 teaspoon | 5 ml | |
| 1 tablespoon | 15 ml | |
| ¼ cup | 60 ml | 2 fl.oz. |
| ⅓ cup | 75 ml | 2½ fl.oz. |
| ½ cup | 125 ml | 4 fl.oz. |
| ⅔ cup | 150 ml | 5 fl.oz. (¼ pint) |
| ¾ cup | 175 ml | 6 fl.oz. |
| 1 cup | 250 ml | 8 fl.oz. |

WEIGHT EQUIVALENTS:

| Imperial | Metric |
| --- | --- |
| 1 oz. | 25 g |
| 2 oz. | 50 g |
| 3 oz. | 75 g |
| 4 oz. | 125 g |
| 5 oz. | 150 g |
| 6 oz. | 175 g |
| 7 oz. | 200 g |
| 8 oz. (½ lb.) | 250 g |
| 9 oz. | 275 g |
| 10 oz. | 300 g |
| 11 oz. | 325 g |
| 12 oz. | 375 g |
| 13 oz. | 400 g |
| 14 oz. | 425 g |
| 15 oz. | 475 g |
| 16 oz. (1 lb.) | 500 g |
| 2 1b. | 1 kg |

MEASUREMENTS:

| Inches | Cm |
| --- | --- |
| ¼ inch | 5 mm |
| ½ inch | 1 cm |
| ¾ inch | 1.5 cm |
| 1 inch | 2.5 cm |
| 2 inches | 5 cm |
| 3 inches | 7 cm |
| 4 inches | 10 cm |
| 5 inches | 12 cm |
| 6 inches | 15 cm |
| 7 inches | 18 cm |
| 8 inches | 20 cm |
| 9 inches | 23 cm |
| 10 inches | 25 cm |
| 11 inches | 28 cm |
| 12 inches | 30 cm |

OVEN TEMPERATURES:

| 225°F | 110°C | Gas ¼ |
| --- | --- | --- |
| 250°F | 120°C | Gas ½ |
| 275°F | 140°C | Gas 1 |
| 300°F | 150°C | Gas 2 |
| 325°F | 160°C | Gas 3 |
| 350°F | 180°C | Gas 4 |
| 375°F | 190°C | Gas 5 |
| 400°F | 200°C | Gas 6 |
| 425°F | 220°C | Gas 7 |
| 450°F | 230°C | Gas 8 |
| 475°F | 240°C | Gas 9 |